# Dona Z. Meilach

# Plant Hangers

## Ideas and Techniques

Macramé, Weaving, Twining,
Coiling, Leather, Antiques, and more

Photos by Dona and Mel Meilach

CROWN PUBLISHERS, INC., NEW YORK

Inquiries should be addressed to Crown Publishers, Inc., One Park Avenue, New York, N.Y. 10016.
Printed in the United States of America
Published simultaneously in Canada by General Publishing Company Limited

Design Consultant: Dona Z. Meilach
Book Design: Huguette Franco

**Library of Congress Cataloging in Publication Data**

Meilach, Dona Z.
  Plant hangers.

  Includes index.
  1.  Plant hangers.  2.  Macramé.  3.  Hand weaving.  I.  Title.
SB418.4.M44  1977       745.59'3       76–58406
ISBN 0–517–52924–6
ISBN 0–517–52925–4 pbk.

## ART-CRAFT BOOKS BY DONA Z. MEILACH

**MACRAMÉ**

Macramé Accessories
Macramé: Creative Design in Knotting

**FIBERS AND FABRICS**

Contemporary Batik and Tie-Dye
Contemporary Leather
Creating Art From Fibers and Fabrics
Creative Stitchery
   with Lee Erlin Snow
Making Contemporary Rugs and Wall Hangings
A Modern Approach to Basketry with Fibers and Grasses
Soft Sculpture and Other Soft Art Forms
Weaving Off-Loom
   with Lee Erlin Snow

**SCULPTURE**

Contemporary Art with Wood
Contemporary Stone Sculpture
Creating Art with Bread Dough
Creating Modern Furniture
Creating Small Wood Objects as Functional Sculpture
Creating with Plastic
Creative Carving
Decorative and Sculptural Ironwork
Direct Metal Sculpture
Sculpture Casting
   with Dennis Kowal
Soft Sculpture and Other Soft Art Forms

**COLLAGE-PAPER**

Accent on Crafts
Box Art: Assemblage and Construction
Collage and Assemblage
   with Elvie Ten Hoor
Collage and Found Art
   with Elvie Ten Hoor
Creating Art from Anything
Papercraft
Papier-mâché Artistry
Printmaking

**DESIGN**

The Artist's Eye
How to Create Your Own Designs
   with Jay and Bill Hinz

**ALSO:**

The Art of Belly Dancing
   with Dahlena
Jazzercise
   with Judi Missett

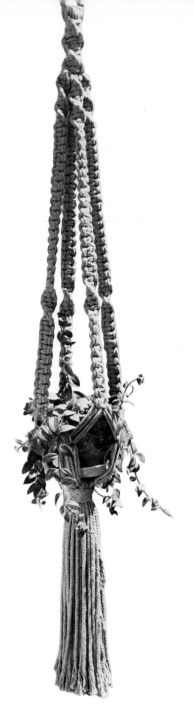

# Acknowledgments

My thanks to the enthusiastic response of macramé addicts, weavers, sculptors, and other artists who shared their creative outpourings with me. Many of the plant hanger examples shown were created especially for this volume by people throughout the country. Others were discovered hanging at art-craft fairs, in homes, model apartments, plant shops, and galleries. My sincere thanks to everyone who said "yes" when we asked for examples to be created, or permission to photograph their work. To those who took the time and effort to photograph their own pieces and share the photos with me, a special thank you. We know how the long, dangling pieces that move in the slightest current defy photographic efforts and often are difficult to display on backgrounds that do not distract. Limited space and lack of good photographic definition prevent using more of the hundreds of examples that were considered.

My thanks to Stanley Siou of Stanislaus Imports, San Francisco. The idea for the book germinated while we were discussing macramé over dinner one evening. He provided much of the cord and beads used in several of the pieces made exclusively for the book. Thanks too, to William Ujifusa, Due South Imports, Inc., Irvine, California. When he heard I was writing the book, he invited me to go through the racks and "take what I needed" to make plant hangers. The wildly wonderful wood, ceramic, porcelain, and other beads displayed in chapter one made me feel like the female version of Captain Queeg.

My gratitude award is offered to Zora Ray for her good taste in selecting plant hangers for her fiber gallery, The Golden Fleece, Laguna, California. She permitted us to photograph woven, knotted, twined, and other pieces, often disrupting the gallery by setting up ladders, then breaking pots and nipping off plant tendrils.

A special thank you to Rick Geary for his drawings used in various chapters, to Collette Russell for helping with correspondence and keeping the photo records straight, and to Marilyn Regula for her splendid job of typing the final manuscript.

A special "I don't know what I'd do without you" bow to my husband, Dr. Melvin Meilach, for invaluable assistance with the photography, for rigging up a portable Rube Goldberg device for suspending the heavy potted pieces in what looks like midair in many of the photos. I'm not sure how to acknowledge my editor Brandt Aymar for his continuing puns and punishment that help to make the preparation of these books almost as much fun as they are work.

Dona Meilach
San Diego

Note: All photos by Dona and Mel Meilach unless otherwise credited.

# Contents

# Introduction: Hang It All

A few years ago plants were displayed mainly at table and floor heights and were viewed from the top or from a frontal position. Today, plants also hang at eye level and above in a dizzying profusion. The hanging plant has become an important decorating device that utilizes space in homes in the corner of a room, in front of a window, and over furniture. It is appearing as never before in restaurants, hotel lobbies, offices, and other public places. Dangly plants and small showy plants that shoot tendrils into the air are becoming mini-gardens in space. To hang these mini-gardens attractively, one needs hangers and pots.

What is responsible for the increasing appeal of aerial gardens? Without question, macramé, the art of decorative knot tying, is the culprit. As people recognized the attractive aspect of plants hanging in space, they explored the potential of macramé as the method for hanging them. Inevitably, the hanger itself became as important as the plant it was designed to display.

As a result an industry developed based on letting plants hang out everywhere. Wood and metal rings, beads and baubles, hooks, and other devices to use with the knotted cords were quickly developed. Potters created vases—some with rounded bottoms to sit into a knotted sling, others with special handles, holes, and knobs for mounting the cords directly to the pots. Importers began to market hangers made with sparsely knotted lengths of cords and a few beads—designs that could be easily mass-produced by inexpensive labor in various countries. Pattern books appeared for making plant hangers. By following explicit instructions people learned how to fashion the basic two knots of macramé into myriad combinations; they created lovely hangers by copying ideas developed by various designers.

Macramé enthusiasts are quick to point out that the procedures are so simple it is easy to look at a finished knotted piece and reproduce a reasonable replica of it without knot-by-knot patterns. If it isn't exact, so much the better; the creator feels an essence of individual creativity which may inject him with the desire and confidence to make entire pieces from his own design.

It is with this urge to create one-of-a-kind individually designed pieces that the plant hangers in this book are offered. They are there for you to adapt and duplicate as you like but, preferably, to use as a point of departure for your own ideas. As you study the examples, you will observe that techniques in addition to macramé are shown. Why? Because creative people do not want to feel cramped, or hemmed in by the necessity of using only one technique.

*Opposite:*
Plant hangers can be imaginatively varied as you will observe when you analyze them individually. The silhouette differs when hoops are used as in the hanger top (*left*), or when lengths of knotted cords begin from the hanging device (*center*), or when the piece is woven (*right*). Hangers left to right by Linda Fosdick, Betté Hughes, Laurie Daniells. *Photographed at The Golden Fleece, Laguna Beach, California*

They feel that if they have an idea for a hanger, it doesn't have to be macramé; it can be entirely another method or it can combine other methods with macramé. Therefore, many examples utilize a variety of techniques for manipulating fibers and fabrics such as weaving, wrapping, stuffing, batik, tie-dye, basketry, crochet, lacemaking, netting, and so forth. General techniques are offered so you can become familiar with and use them. For more complex techniques such as batik and tie-dye that limited space prevents showing, refer to the suggested book list on page 94.

Remember that making a plant hanger does not require "fit" as does a knitted sweater. If the hanger is slightly longer than anticipated, adjust it by tying more knots, cutting cords and reknotting, or by shortening it at the ceiling. If a piece is too short, lengths can be decoratively added on; sometimes a second pot sling can be suspended beneath.

When you create hangers that are individually your own design and approach, you are always free to improvise, revise, and finally boast with justifiable pride and honesty, "I made it myself."

**ABOUT FIBERS**   The majority of plant hangers shown in the book, with the exception of those in chapter 4, are composed mainly of fibers. The variety of choices of available fibers to use for your plant hangers can be formidable at first. But all fibers have characteristic appearances and qualities for working them and for permanence under certain conditions. They fall into basic categories discussed below.

For any major project, it is wise to develop a sample of the knotting (or other technique employed) in different fibers to determine how they look and how much stretch will be incurred after a few weeks with the weight of a potted plant in it. Hangers to be placed out of doors should be made of materials that will endure the elements of a particular climate. Many of the dyed cords fade and deteriorate in time when exposed to sunny, humid conditions. A jute plant hanger may last only one or two years on an outdoor porch overlooking the sea, but indoors, it can last several years.

The fiber you select will also depend on how big the hanger will be and how heavy a plant it may support. Thick cords lend themselves to large, dramatic hangings, sometimes with two or three pots suspended. Thin cords can be worked into small hangers used with delicate plants in small rooms or limited spaces. The lighting to be used on the hanger should be considered when deciding on shiny or dull materials. Spotlights playing on plants and hangers can enhance them and throw interesting shadows on walls and ceilings.

All fibers are made from plants, animals, and synthetics. Plant fibers are considered vegetable fibers: cotton from the cotton shrub, linen from flax, jute from the jute plant, and hemp from the hemp plant. Sisal and henequen are derived from agave plants. Each has a characteristic texture and appearance. Sisal is rough and scratchy, jutes are softer and more pliable than sisal.

Animal fibers include those made from the fur and hair of animals such as wool from sheep, alpaca from llamas, yak hair from yaks, mohair from goats, camel's hair from camels, silk from silkworms, and so forth.

Synthetics are man-made fibers available in an incredible variety. They are made from chemical compounds; probably the best recognized synthetic fiber is rayon. Synthetics most

Cotton, linen, jute, waxed nylon, leather, cotton web cord, roving, sisal, and novelty yarns are available in a staggering assortment of textures, sizes, and colors, all adaptable to attractive plant hangers.

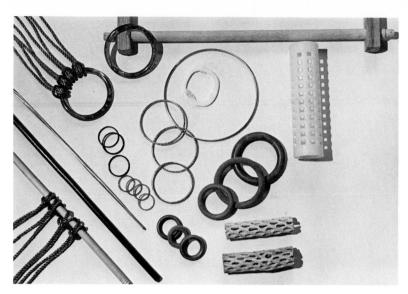

often used in plant hangings are rayon, nylon, polyolefin, and polypropylene.

The preparation of fibers for the market begins with cleaning and carding the raw material, then twisting and pulling it into a long strand, called "roving," in preparation for spinning. Roving is soft and pliable and pulls apart easily but it is often sold for creating special effects within a woven or knotted hanger. The yarn or fiber is spun from roving into individual strands. Each strand is called a ply. Most rope, cord, string, and so forth is composed of several strands, or plies, for strength.

The thickness of a cord is measured in two ways—the thickness of an individual ply and the number of these plies. The larger the plies, the larger a number the cord is given. The more plies per rope, the thicker it is. A #72-5 ply rope will be appreciably thicker than a #48-5 ply.

Some manufacturers also list cords by the overall thickness, measured in the circumference, by millimeters. Jute and sisal especially, will be labeled with such markings as 2mm, 5 ply; or 5mm, 4 ply. The thicker the diameter and the more plies, the heavier the cord. See Cord Chart, page 94.

Cords for a specific project should, if possible, be purchased at one time. The nature of the materials, the manufacturing process, and the sources cause color dye lots, the thickness and quality of the cords, to differ from time to time. This is especially true of animal and vegetable materials. Two packages of jute with the same label, purchased a few months apart, can differ appreciably in color or texture so that when they are worked into one plant hanger, the difference can be obvious and detract from the desired appearance of the finished piece.

**HANGING DEVICES**   When plant hangers first appeared on the market, they were generally hung by a piece of rope attached to a hardware store hook. As their popularity and complexity increased, manufacturers developed a line of decorative hooks that offer several conveniences. The hooks themselves swivel so the grower can rotate the plants toward the light at a finger's touch. Some have pulley systems so they can be raised and lowered for watering or to give the plant a better position in relation to available light. Many are available in antique brass, wrought iron, and gold finishes.

The plant hanger itself must be designed so it will hold onto the hook. For this purpose finished and unfinished

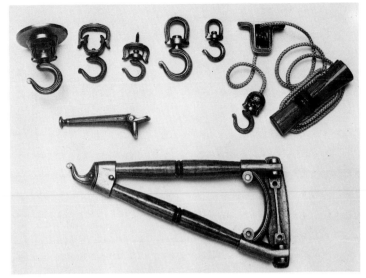

wood and metal rings are available from craft distributors. Decorative and colorful rings are usually left exposed. Plain rings are integrated into the design of the hanging by covering them with wrapped or knotted cords. Often, a sennit (length of knotted cords) is folded over to become the hanging loop. Observe the different types of beginnings in the illustrated items throughout the book and especially the details in chapter 2, pages 26 to 35.

Metal rings are suggested for heavy hangings as wood may break in time from the weight of the plant and pot. Metal rings are sold in different gauges and diameters from ⅝ inch to 2¼ inches and larger. Finishes are gilt, nickel, antique brass, and bronze. Hardwood rings range from ½ inch to 2 inches in diameter. Rattan rings range from 4 inches to 25 inches in diameter. These larger diameter rattan rings are usually used within the body of the hanging and not where they will have to support the entire weight of the piece.

Dowel rods can be purchased from hardware and lumber suppliers. They should be thick enough to support the hanger and potted plant without eventually bending. They are recommended only for lightweight hangings. Ends can be finished with finials. Dowels should be painted or stained before working them into the hangings.

Sunhook plant hanging hardware includes a locking planter pulley with a nylon cord in a cord storing pull handle. The swivel hook enables the grower to lower plants to ideal positions for watering and tending without having to remove the planter from its hook. *Photos, courtesy, HOMECRAFT Division of Gries Reproducer Co., New Rochelle, N.Y.*

11

Plastic rings are not as sturdy as metal or wood, but can be used for small plants and for interior sections where negative areas or wrapped circles may be desired.

Found objects may be beautifully adapted to hanging plants. These may include driftwood, tree branches, picture frame molding, root forms, bones, and shells. Often the item itself will suggest the design.

**DESIGNING AND WORKING TIPS**

When you decide you want to create a plant hanger, how do you begin? Where do you find ideas for the designs? the shapes? the colors? How do you know which materials go well together?

Without meaning to appear vague or cryptic, the practical, realistic answer is: you begin the best way that works for you. You have to jump in, experiment, expect some trial and error. Soon everything will begin to work together for you. This is the essence of the creative act. The following should help make your creative juices flow.

A. When you are familiar with macramé, weaving, basketry, and so forth, your vocabulary of these techniques will help stimulate ideas. You will know what you can do with the basic knots of macramé, for example. By observing other plant hangers, and how different details are used, you can begin to think of combining the details into an overall hanging that is uniquely your own design. For this reason, specific patterns for making individual pieces are not offered in this book. Rather, the hangers are shown so that you can see the range of possible combinations, select those you like, and put them together in your own way. A macramé shorthand (page 17) will make it easy to visualize and combine different elements in a design.

B. Often your materials will suggest your design. A ball of natural jute can be developed into many of the knotted hangers illustrated. But if you happen to pick up a special on seine twine, you might look for a hanger that is smaller, narrower, and more delicate than one made in jute.

C. Sometimes, the linear design on a specific pot will trigger an idea for the hanger. You might like to repeat some of the pot's lines in the hanger as Ursy Leuder did in the hanger on page 61.

D. Many people begin working and let the design evolve as they work. It would be impossible to develop specific directions for Gary Cline's wrapped pieces (p. 60 and color section). The intricately wrapped and twisted cords are worked in and around one another as the hanger evolves.

E. The overall shape of the hanger is often determined by the space to be filled. If you want to put a plant high in a corner, a short, wide bottomed hanger may fit better than a long skinny hanger. Always consider the outer silhouette of the hanger and then think about how you want to fill it in.

F. When you design, think of the pot to be placed in the hanger, but think, too, if the hanger would be more attractive with a tray, a basket, a glass circle, or square, or a wood box, and plan the holding portion of the planter accordingly.

Color in plant hangers is a personal matter. Some people contend that the hanger should be monotone and not detract from the showy plants. Others believe the hanger should be intricate and elegant and the plant incidental to the hanger. Available colors of cords can temper your decision about color; but even then you have great latitutde because fibers can be colored with household dyes. Perhaps the beads you want to use within the hanger can

Wood beads (*above*), ceramic and glass beads, and seashells (*left*) are among the stunning variety of colorful, attractive beads made specifically for fiber projects. They are designed with holes large enough to string onto heavy cords and are ideal for macramé and other fiber hangers. *Beads, courtesy, Due South Imports, Irvine, California, and Stanislaus Imports, San Francisco*

help you determine a single color or a combination of colors. If you have predominantly yellow beads, you might want to make a yellow plant hanger or contrast them against brown. Stained dark wood beads can be used with dark jutes to blend in; or with white cotton to contrast.

Some people plan their hangings using a "head, body, and tail" concept. The "head" is the top portion of the hanging, the "body" is the central portion with the pot cradle at the bottom, the "tail" is the bottom trim—tassels and fringe—and they proportion these so that the head and tail are subordinate to the body. The "body" is designed to be the most interesting portion of the hanger where dramatic detailing is accomplished.

# Macramé

2

More plant hangers are made with macramé knots than by any other method. When other techniques are used, some knotting may also be required for beginning or ending a piece. Embellishments used for macramé, such as adding beads, wrapping, and tassels, are used in the other fiber procedures, so the majority of instructions are presented in this chapter. Weaving, basketry, and non-macramé methods are demonstrated in chapter 3 and accompany the examples where shown.

Macramé is deceptively easy to do, even when the results appear complex. There are only two basic knots: the Clove Hitch and the Square Knot, which can be worked in different progressions. A few decorative knots are added for fun and variety. After you tie the knots and familiarize yourself with the appearance of each one, you can quickly "read" how a hanging is made and emulate it closely. It is like learning an alphabet with only a few letters.

With this alphabet concept in mind, a macramé shorthand has been developed (page 17). You can literally look at a macramé work, jot down the knots and decorative additions in the shorthand, and have a design you can copy or work from. Use the shorthand to analyze and, if you like, imitate, a few of the hangers in this book, then begin to design your own. Where cradles are covered with plants, you can visualize a logical follow-through for the arrangement after only a little practice. You can adapt a knot arrangement from a photo of another pot or improvise your own.

When you begin to plan your own designs you might select the head from one piece, the body from another, and the tail from a third. Using the shorthand, you'll know immediately how they will relate to one another and what changes, if any, you should make to improve upon and coordinate the parts.

For greater precision, you can scale a hanger to a desired size by planning it on graph paper. Knot a sample length of the cord so you can determine how many Square Knots, for example, there will be to an inch. Then figure the length you want the finished piece to be and graph your design accordingly.

As you analyze the construction of a plant hanger decide whether the piece would be more efficiently and logically worked from the head down or from under the pot cradle up toward the head.

This analysis will become easy after you learn the knots and study the examples and construction details illustrated. You can also analyze those hangers that may have been worked as one piece or as two separate sections assembled. Working portions separately, then putting them together, builder fashion, is used for pieces where one holder is

*Opposite:*
An easy-to-create design with the basic macramé knots in white cotton seine twine enhances the corner of a breakfast room with wood plank walls. It has the feeling of "bringing the outdoors in." Two rings and two dowels are used with the Josephine Knot suspended in the ring and Half Knot Twists worked below. A tassel is used for the tail. *Collection, Dr. and Mrs. Robert Malkus, La Mesa, California*

Basic macramé supplies include a knotting board or foam pillow into which T pins can be pushed to hold the knots in place. T pins, ruler, scissors, bars or rings for mounting the cords, glue, and plastic straws (optional). The macramé board may be marked off with horizontal and vertical lines 1″ apart to help keep the knotting straight. When the work is under way, the ring can be placed on a hook in a wall or ceiling and the knotting progresses without the board and pinning. Spring clip clothespins are useful as extra "hands" to hold knots in place.

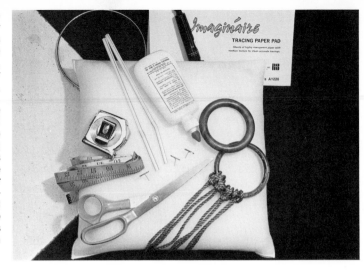

suspended within the circumference of an outer structure. Some pieces are purposely designed so one pot can hang within another and be removed or so new sections can be added on.

## HOW MUCH CORD TO USE?

The unknown factor in macramé is the amount of cord you will need for a specific project. The general rule is to figure that each finished length of knotted cord requires four times the amount of unknotted cord. This will vary depending upon how many tightly woven knots you will need compared with lengths of floating cords (unknotted lengths). The general formula is:

Determine how many lengths of knotting you will use and the finished length each knotted cord will be. Then multiply:

Length of finished hanging × number of knotted strands × 4 = the total yardage required.

Note: When doubling the mounted cord using the center of each cord for the Lark's Head, figure that *each cord length is to be cut eight times the length you want the finished piece to be,* not *the four times used to determine total amount of cord required.*

For greater accuracy, knot and measure a sample length. If you're going to make a sennit of Square Knots, tie four knots, then untie and measure the length of the cord used. You now know how much cord is required for four knots. If you plan on sixteen knots, for example, you will need four times the known length for that sennit.

In the same way you can calculate how much cord you will need for a Josephine Knot, floating lengths, wrapping, etc. Always notate these measurements on an index card with a sketch of the plant hanger and the size and manufacturer of the cord used. You can determine how closely you came to your projected requirements. You will have it for future reference should you want to duplicate the hanger.

## REPAIRS

The wise plant grower will place a potted plant with a drain hole within a decorative solid bottom pot. The not-so-cautious person will place the draining planted pot directly on the cords. In time, moisture from the plant can deteriorate the fibers which may require replacement or repair. Always retain some of the original cord for repairs, which can be made by cutting out worn portions and adding new sections by splicing, wrapping in with matching twine, and gluing with a waterproof household cement. The repaired area can be wrapped with waterproof duct tape. Or before the repair is made, string a length of tube plastic or a plastic straw on the cord, make the repair, then slip the plastic over it. Plastic tubing in different diameters can be bought where aquarium supplies are sold or in do-it-yourself centers.

Macramé shorthand is simply a device for you to use so you can quickly notate how a hanger is made when you see one. You may not repeat it exactly, but you will have the general knotting progression and numbers of cords. Before you actually begin knotting, you may wish to work the design on graph paper so you can judge the number of knots needed for a given length. After you know how many knots there are to an inch of the cord you will be using it will help you to estimate the yardage needed.

## MACRAMÉ SHORTHAND

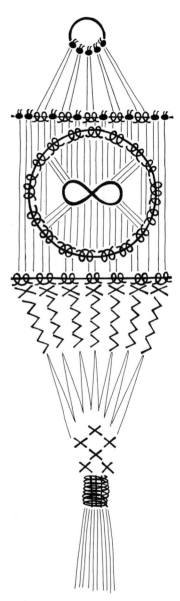

| | |
|---|---|
| 🬀 | Lark's Head |
| ℓℓ | Clove Hitch |
| 🬀🬀 | Clove Hitching on a ring |
| 🬀🬀 | Clove Hitch on a horizontal bar |
| 🬀 🬀 | Clove Hitch on a specific angle |
| 🬀🬀 | Vertical Clove Hitch |
| ℓ | Half Hitch |
| ✕ | Square Knot |
| ✕✕ ✕✕ | Alternating Square Knot |
| ⟩ | Half-Knot Twist |
| 🬀🬀⟩⟩ | Square Knot Button |
| ⦀ | Floating (unknotted) cord |
| ⚏ | Chains—select and use the necessary symbol for a specific chain |
| 🬀 | Alternating Clove Hitch |
| ⦚ | Exchanging knotters and anchors |
| ▦ | Wrapping |
| ⋔ | Tassel |
| ❜ | Overhand Knot |
| o | Bead addition |
| ⦚⦚ | Fraying |
| ∞ | Josephine Knot |

A shorthand analysis of the hanger on page 14 would look like this and be very easy to follow.

Make up your own symbols for any other knots or detailing you will use. A similar shorthand can be developed for weaving, basketry, and other techniques, too.

## BASIC MACRAMÉ PROCEDURES

The principle of macramé is to interknot lengths of cords. For working convenience think of them as placing knotting cords over "anchor" or "filler" cords. The knotting cords are folded over another cord, a bar, or ring and then worked in the methods illustrated. Sennits are lengths of knotted cords. Floating cords are unknotted portions within a sennit. Note: Directions in different books can refer to the same knots by different names.

## The Lark's Head

The Lark's Head is the basic method for mounting the cord to a bar or ring. The cord is doubled and looped as shown.

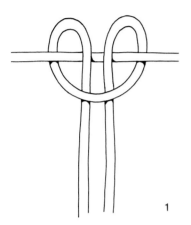
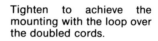

1

2

3

### Lark's Head Mounting

Place central bend of the cord under the holding bar; with the bend at the bottom bring the ends over the bar and under the loop.

Tighten to achieve the mounting with the loop over the doubled cords.

### Reverse Lark's Head

The Reverse Lark's Head results in the loop behind the two cords. Place the folded cord under the bar with the bend at the top; fold over and pull the loose cords through the bend. Tighten.

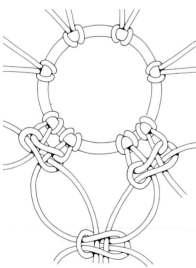

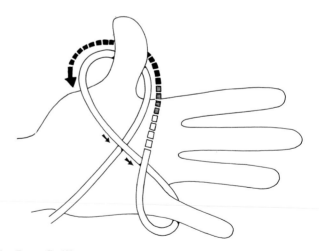

### The Butterfly Wrap

The Lark's Head is often mounted on a ring, then worked into rows of Square Knots.

Bundling the long working cords into butterflies can simplify the knotting procedure. Wind the cord as shown and secure with a rubber band around the bundle; then pull the bundle to free the cord as you need it.

The Clove Hitch (also called the Double Half Hitch) is the first basic macramé knot. The knotting cord is looped twice over the anchor cord (or rod or ring). It may be tied in horizontal, vertical, and diagonal directions. It can be worked from right to left and from left to right. The direction of the anchor determines the direction of the knotted pattern.

## The Clove Hitch

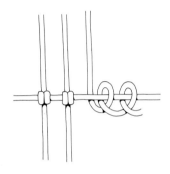

### The Horizontal Clove Hitch

The anchor is held taut horizontally *over* the knotting cords. Each knotting cord is looped over the anchor and then under the anchor and tightened to appear as shown in the finished knots.

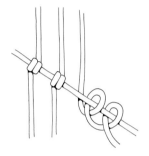

### The Diagonal Clove Hitch

The same knots placed on an anchor cord held taut on an angle will result in angles and diamond shaped designs within the hangers. Knots should be tight and even so the linear design will be clear.

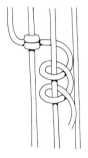

### The Vertical Clove Hitch

The same knot worked vertically uses one length of cord for tying all the knots and each strand of knotting cord changes its role and becomes an anchor as the knotting cord is tied over it.

### The Half Hitch

Only one loop of the Clove Hitch results in the Half Hitch. Knots may be made over one or over multiple anchor cords.

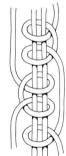

### Clove Hitch Chains

Sennits can be made with Clove Hitches and with Half Hitches worked from the left or the right of the anchor cords.

### Lark's Head Chain

For variety, the Lark's Head can also be tied over series of anchor cords in chainlike sennits.

## The Square Knot

The Square Knot is the second basic macramé knot; its versatility is incredible. It is generally tied with four strands using the two outside strands for knotting, the two inside strands as anchors. It can, of course, utilize as many cords for anchors or knotting as you like; the more cords, the thicker the sennits.

**A**        **B**        **C**        **D**

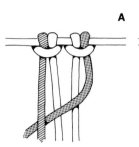
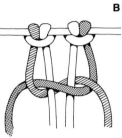
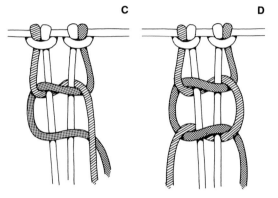

### The Square Knot

A. Bring the right cord *over* and to the left of the two center cords (anchors) and place the left cord *over* the right.

B. Bring the left cord *under* the right, *behind* the anchors and *through* the loop formed by the right cord and then *over* the right cord.

C. Repeat same procedure from the other side: Place the left cord *over* the anchors and the right cord *over* the left.

D. Place the right *under* the left, *behind* the anchors and *through* the loop formed by the left cord and *over* the left cord. Pull each half of the knot tight to result in the completed Square Knot.

### The Alternating Square Knot

Combining the right half of one group of cords with the left half of the adjacent group to form a new set of cords results in the Alternating Square Knot pattern shown in drawings (*right*) and in an actual cord (*below*). Throughout the book observe the different numbers of cords used in alternating progressions, in solidly and loosely tied areas, and in designs that move from one side to another.

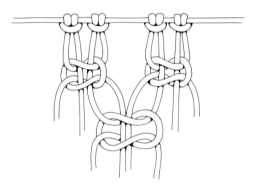

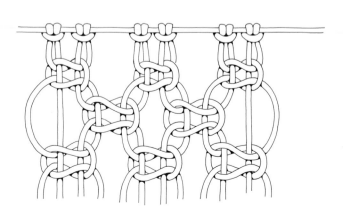

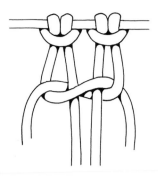

## Half Knot and Half Knot Twist

The Half Knot is only one half of the Square Knot which can be used by itself. However, when several Half Knots are made in progression, they twist around the anchors. The knots must be tied tightly.

A succession of Half Knot Twists results in . . .

. . . a twisted sennit with this appearance.

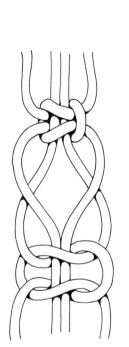

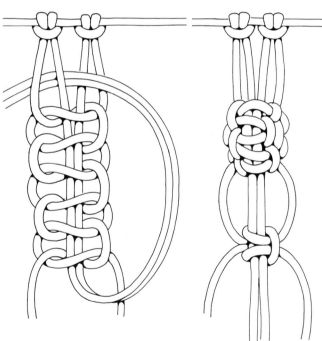

## Exchanging Anchors and Knotters

For variety and color changes, a Square Knot variation consists of switching anchors and knotters.

## Square Knot Button

The button is made by tying three or more Square Knots and pulling them up into a loop by inserting the anchors over the first Square Knot. All the cords move up to form the button and the knotting cords are brought down from the back and continue to be used for another button or for a continuation of Square Knot sennits.

**OTHER KNOTS**

A select few additional knots are employed in a macramé repertoire because of their versatility and practicality for plant hangers. There is no limit to the numbers of decorative knots that can be used; literally hundreds can be found in sailors' manuals of knots.

**The Chinese Crown Knot**

A sennit of finished Chinese Crown Knots tied in cotton seine twine with two strands in each of four knotting groups.

When tied one over another the Chinese Crown Knot is well suited to plant hangers. It is usually begun using the cords mounted over a ring, or with cords folded at the top to provide a loop for attaching to a hook. There are several ways to tie the knot; the one illustrated is easy to follow; when you understand the principle you can work it any way you prefer.

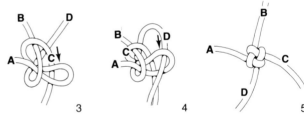

**Chinese Crown Knot**

Begin with the cords divided into four groups (or four individual cords) separated as shown. Assign a "label" to each cord. Then:

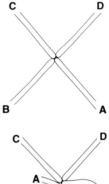

(1) Place cord A over the center and between B and C, leaving a loop as shown.

(2) Place cord B over cord A at the center between C and D but pull the loop close in to the center. All cords except A should be pulled tight to the center.

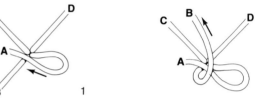

(3) Bring cord C across center over cord B and between D and A.

(4) Bring cord D through the loop formed by cord A.

(5) Pull each cord tight to form the finished Chinese Crown Knot.

---

**The Overhand and Coil Knots**

The Overhand Knot is used to tie at cord ends to prevent fraying. It can be tied with one or any number of cords in single or multiple arrangements.

When several Overhand Knots are placed within a loop, the ends are pulled to result . . .

. . . in the Coil Knot which is decorative and also useful for ends and for keeping beads on strands.

Designs incorporating Josephine Knots within centers of rings or for sennits can be studied in the examples throughout the book to give you an idea for their placement. The knots can be made with single, double, or multiple strands. When multiple strands are used, they must be placed carefully so they lie flat.

## The Josephine Knot

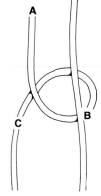 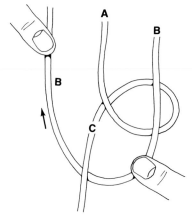

### Josephine Knot

Assign letters to the cord parts as shown. Place B over the loop made by the left cord, A.

Hold B and bring it under part C.

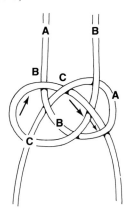  

Continue to bring B over A, under C, over B, and under A.

Work the cords around so they are even and then repeat if desired.

A Josephine Knot worked with doubled cords.

---

Tassels are used extensively for finishing the tail of the pot.

## Tassels

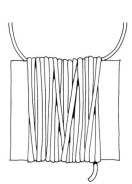 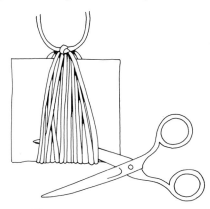 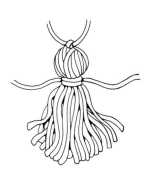

### Tassels

Wrap cords around a piece of stiff cardboard the length you want the tassel to be. Place a tie cord at the top under the wrap.

Tie the cord at the top tightly to bundle the tassel and cut the bottom with scissors.

Wrap another length of cord down about 1 inch or more (depending upon the tassel length) and tie tightly.

**MORE TECHNIQUES** Gathering and wrapping cords is essential for ending cords and for grouping them within the sennits. Sometimes you will wrap with one of the knotting cords as shown in the first wrapping method (left). Or you may prefer to use the Peruvian wrap (right) for wrapping with an added cord of another or the same color.

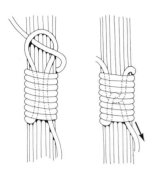

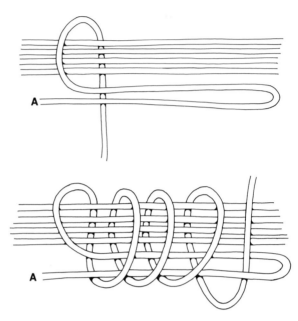

To wrap cords using one of the lengths in the sennit, form a loop with one end of the cord and hold the bottom secure. Wrap the cord around all and place the end through the loop. Pull down on the loop pulling the end inside. Clip off any loose ends.

Introduce a new length of cord parallel to the lengths you want to gather in the wrap. Lay out as shown, *above. Below,* wrap the cord around all the strands and pull the strand (A) which will bring the loop and the loose end under the wraps. The wrapping should be done very tightly (it is only drawn loosely for demonstration).

**Spiral Clove Hitch**
Use this for a tassel or for the beginning of a small plant hanger. Fold the cords in half and use an anchor cord about 3 times as long as the knotting cords. Hold the anchor at an angle and begin to Clove Hitch with each strand. Continue holding the anchor about 1 inch below the row before it so the movement spirals down the cords. Finish with two rows of Horizontal Clove Hitches. Finish the knotting ends with Overhand Knots or add beads.

Square Knotting from a ring can be used for beginning a pot hanger from the bottom up. The ring becomes the center bottom on which the pot sits and the knotting expands outward to become the pot's cradle. The cords are gathered above the pot, in necessary groupings for sennits, and are finished at the top hook with a gathering knot. Hangers can be started from the bottom this way and assembled to portions that begin at the top by knotting them together in interesting designs.

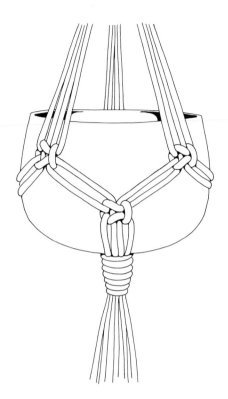

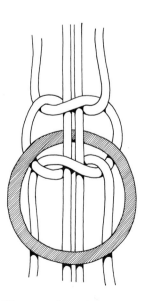

Unraveled plies can be an attractive ending for unknotted lengths of cords and for tassels. Simply unwind the plies and fluff them out. You can use a wire brush or a comb for additional texturing.

The pot sling, or cradle, should surround the circumference of the pot with at least three sets of strands. The sennits are divided evenly and the left half of one set of cords is knotted with the right set of the adjacent group and slightly lower in the same way that Alternating Square Knots are worked. It often helps to tape the cords to the pot with masking tape so you can space them evenly.

## MORE WORKING HINTS

To make macramé even easier, discover your own shortcuts as you proceed. The following are tried and true solutions to some of the working problems.

A. If you mix up knotting lengths and anchor cords, place a tiny knot, rubber band, or colored bead on the anchor cord end for quick identity.

B. When ends of synthetic cords such as nylon, polypropylene, and others fray, cut off the frayed section and burn the tightly plied end with a match until a small, hard ball forms and prevents the material from unwinding.

C. When cords become too short too fast, they can be spliced, but the spliced section is never as strong as the single length. To splice, unply about two inches from each end to be butted together and intertwine them tightly. Wrap with another length of thread (you may have to add wraps where there is no splicing to carry out the appearance that it is part of the design). Add white glue over the splice before wrapping.

D. When many beads are to be placed on the knotted lengths, string them to the cord before making a butterfly, then simply push them up as needed and knot into place.

Rings, antique items, and beads may be added onto the anchor cords before the knotting is continued. Here, a ring is placed within the two halves of a Square Knot.

## OFF TO A GOOD START

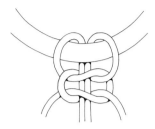

Ways to cover a ring:
Begin with Square Knots all around and use for knotting.

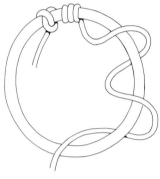

Wrap a plain ring, adding glue on the ring before covering with cord.

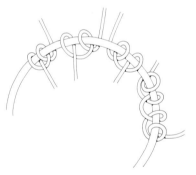

When a ring is added either horizontally or vertically within the body of the work, each knotting cord is brought down around the ring and Clove Hitched in. To fill up a large ring, it may be necessary to wrap one cord around the ring twice as shown at right.

Bill Tasek begins his hanger with a covered ring, then a Square Knotted bundle as shown in the drawings on the following page. The anchor cords are cut and fringed for extra interest and to repeat the tassel and fringe effect on the body ring and the tail. Approx. 7 feet long.

By Mary Rudesill. A trio of 3-ply sisal hangings illustrate a variety of silhouettes and details worked from the same beginning: the Square Knot made over the grouped strands. Finished lengths and working strands are from left to right: 5 feet worked with 10 strands 26 feet long; 5 feet 4 inches worked with 8 strands 26 feet long; 6½ feet worked with 12 strands 30 feet long, plus a 7-inch wire ring and 8 ceramic beads. *Photo, courtesy, artist*

## SQUARE KNOTTED BUNDLE BEGINNING

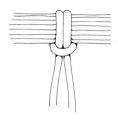

Fold the knotting cords in half. With an extra wrapping cord tie a Lark's Head around the knotting cords about 2 inches left of the center of the fold.

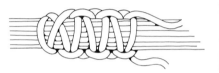

Use the ends from the Lark's Head, cross them over the strands, and tie Square Knots for about 4 inches.

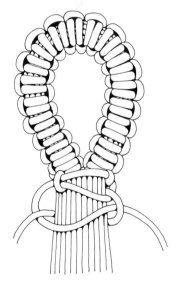

Fold the Square Knotted length in half and then wrap the entire bundle with additional Square Knots. The result is a sturdy loop used for suspending the pot hanger from a ceiling hook.

By Mary Rudesill. Observe the different ideas for ending and for the pot cradle. All are made of 3-ply sisal. The top of the center hanger features Square Knots worked in the round and held with wrapping. *Courtesy, artist*

By Patsy Bordeaux. Soft cotton cable cord made into Square Knots and Half-Knot Twists. The ends of the knotting cords have been combined with extra cords folded over to yield a thick tail ending. *Photographed at The Golden Fleece, Laguna Beach, California*

*Opposite:*

By Tom J. Brunelle. White nylon seine twine is worked from an odd-shaped piece of driftwood using all the protrusions. The shape of the wood is the excuse for working the hanger horizontally as well as in the vertical dimension. *Courtesy, Tom's Green Thumb, Carlsbad, California*

*Opposite:*

*Left:*

By Betté Hughes. Jute worked into Square Knots, Alternating Square Knots, and Half-Knot Twists is combined with ceramic beads, a medallion, and a tree branch. *Photographed at The Golden Fleece, Laguna Beach, California*

*Right:*

An intricately patterned ceramic centerpiece is combined with wooden beads and dowel rods. Note that the original 20 strands mounted on the hanging ring are Clove Hitched onto the first horizontal dowel; 8 additional strands are mounted on each end. The cradle is composed of the same central strands as the heading, which yields a harmonious balance to the composition. *Collection, Dr. and Mrs. Robert Malkus, La Mesa, California*

Objects worked into the body of the plant hanger can be dramatic and different. A ceramic medallion, made with holes large enough to accept Lark's Head mountings, is used with odd-shaped wood pieces. The macramé, almost incidental to the design, is necessary structurally. *Collection, Dr. and Mrs. Robert Malkus, La Mesa, California*

By John Prater. A ball shape of unknotted cord is an unusual counterpoint to the tightly knotted body of the hanger. It can be made by stuffing the center of the gathered cords with scrap pieces of cord or a Styrofoam ball, then wrapping beneath.

32

33

A cornucopia basket by Kit Hughes is made in the round with Square Knots and Spiral and Horizontal Clove Hitches. *Photographed at The Golden Fleece, Laguna Beach, California*

Most knotting "in the round" details are used for the body and top of hangers. Becky Clark cleverly applies the motif for the pot cradle as well. Some are made for individual pots, some are for multiples. The cords are mounted on rings with a diameter slightly larger than that of the pot. Top strands are attached to the rings and worked into the hanger head. The grouped baskets have an architectural quality. *Courtesy, artist*

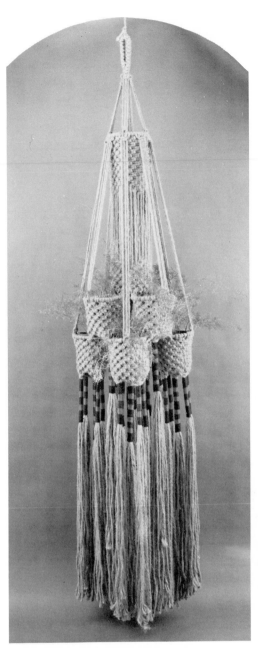

By Becky Clark

By Becky Clark

Bill Johnson's combination screen and plant holder measures 7 feet high, 13 feet 4 inches wide. It is made with 2,800 yards of 9-ply natural jute. It has many things going on in intricate and unusual knotting patterns. A knot-guessing contest subsequently revealed that it has 25,732 knots. *Photo, Bill Johnson Courtesy, Betty Ann's Handcrafts, San Diego, California*

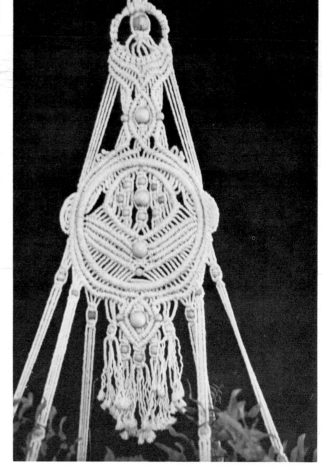

*Detail of hanger on opposite page:* Intricate knotting patterns characterize many of Janet Bleen Reed's plant hangers made with #18 to #24 white cotton seine twine. Covering large rings within the knotting sometimes requires the use of two Clove Hitches made with 1 knotting cord as shown in the drawing on the bottom of page 26. If necessary, extra cords can be added to fill the space around the ring and these cords then used for anchors for the Clove Hitch rows. The finished pot is 36 inches long excluding the tassel. *Photo, Linda Cummens*

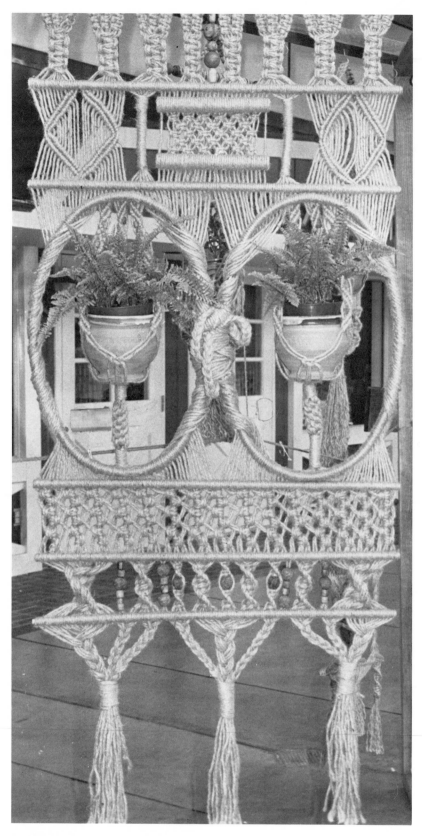

By Marsha Hann. Natural jute with dowels and
oval rings. A plant hanger to be used as a room
divider or window treatment employs different
length and diameter dowels, beads, and ovals.

By Susan Neal. White seine twine. An exciting
use of symmetrical design on each side of a central pot. It has a complex appearance but close
analysis reveals a simple structure using heavy
wood support rods.

Planter curtain by Diane Travis of 4-ply jute
measures 53 inches high and 32 inches wide. The
diamond shape and joining horizontals are
shaped of aluminum wire. *Photo, Alaine Johnson*

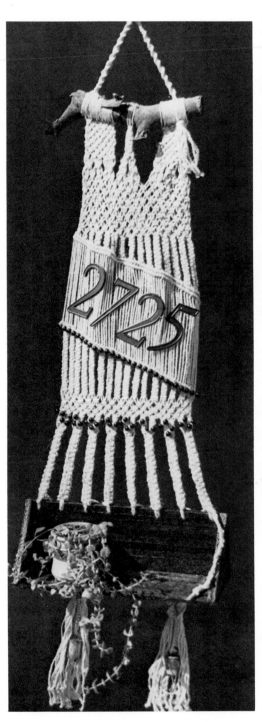

By Mary Baughn. A combination plant hanging shelf and a place for an address is a nice addition next to the front door of the artist's home. Bells, added at the bottom, serve as a wind chime.

Mary Baughn uses dried pine cones for the unusually designed body of a triple plant hanger.

**ASYMMETRICALLY DESIGNED PIECES:**

SEASIDE. Linee Lindquist. Driftwood and shells must be carefully arranged with the pot and its cradle so that the final piece balances structurally even though the design is asymmetrical.

*Opposite:*
AUTUMN TWIST. Judee DuBourdieu. Dark brown and natural jutes with gold handspun yarns. An ornamental gourd is used for the planter. Observe how the wood is used within the hanging instead of as support across the top. 4½ feet high, 1½ feet wide. *Courtesy, artist*

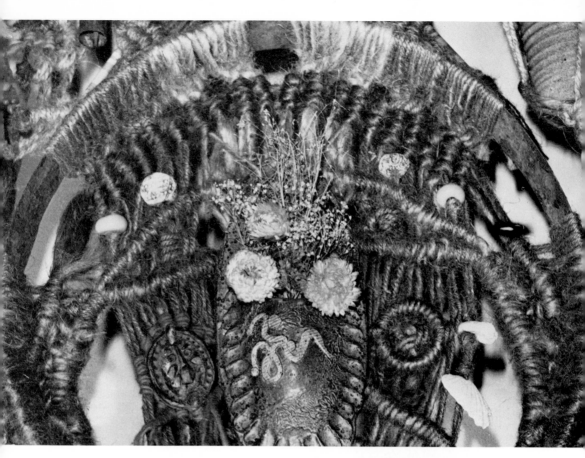

*Detail of hanging (opposite) by Bruce Collings:*
A metal hoop serves as the focal point for the
ceramic weed pot with dried flowers and varied
ceramic beads. The hanger holds three pots for
growing plants, two at the bottom and one at top
right. A piece of odd-shaped wood and ceramic
forms are also worked onto the surface, all suspended from a sturdy branch. *Photographed at
The Golden Fleece, Laguna Beach, California*

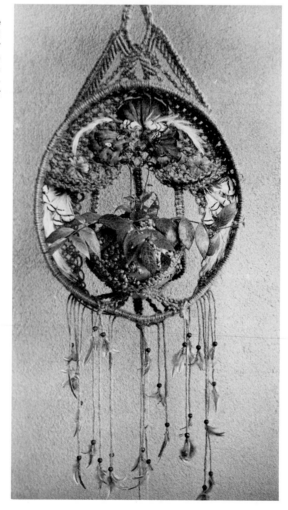

CALIPH. Judee DuBourdieu. Natural jute and
feathers. The circular support is a barrel stay. 3½
feet high, 1½ feet wide. *Courtesy, artist*

By Jan Myers. Natural linen and dark brown waxed linen are knotted from a ring onto a wiggly shaped branch. The clay beads and pots are also made by the artist. *Photo, artist*

Jan Myers uses a woodworker's clamp mounted on the corner of a desk to hold the ring as she works the heading. *Courtesy, artist*

The Macrapole is a tripod based metal stand with adjustable rings; it enables the plant hanger artist to develop horizontal elements so they are even. *Courtesy, Green Gables, Granada Hills, California*

TRYST. Judee DuBourdieu. Brown, natural, and varying shades of melon and orange jute. 4 feet long, 2½ feet wide. The macramé basis is an old jack handle found in the junk heap. A large gourd suspended within holds the plant. *Courtesy, artist*

**INCORPORATING ANTIQUES, FOUND OBJECTS, AND OTHER ITEMS**

Antiques and found objects are becoming a popular adjunct for plant hangers. The example on the previous page by Judee DuBourdieu incorporates a jack handle; Janet Bleen Reed's hanging, right and below, is enhanced by rusty horse hardware. Singletrees used in farming and for harnessing animals together can be used in many creative ways.

One has only to become plant hanger oriented to recognize that objects found at farm auctions, garage sales, and in antique and secondhand stores can be easily visualized as "working" in the composition. Often, the object itself will suggest the design. Wheels, pulleys, barrel parts, machinery parts, gears, metal portions from old buggies, wagons, and what not are all potential supports for simple and intricately worked plant hangers.

Found objects should be well integrated into the hanging with consideration given to the shaping and the colors of the cords used. If rust tends to rub off, the objects can be cleaned with rust remover liquids; or, as Janet Reed prefers, the rust can be fixed beneath a coat of clear acrylic spray so its natural patina is used.

A hanging that incorporates antique pieces should be fitted with a pot that carries out the idea and look of the pieces within.

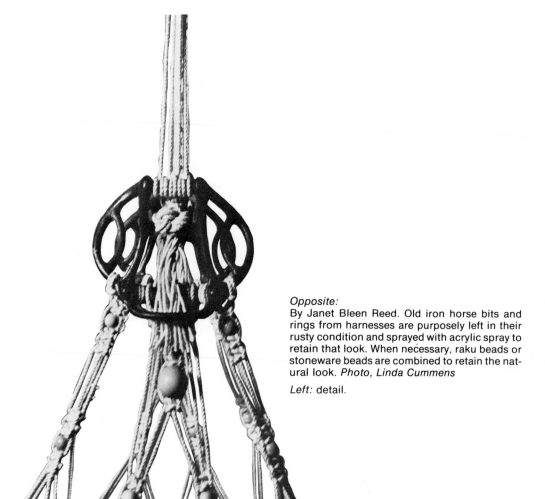

*Opposite:*
By Janet Bleen Reed. Old iron horse bits and rings from harnesses are purposely left in their rusty condition and sprayed with acrylic spray to retain that look. When necessary, raku beads or stoneware beads are combined to retain the natural look. *Photo, Linda Cummens*

*Left:* detail.

By Dee Menagh. Tie-dyed fabric stuffed with foam.

By Dona Meilach. Macramé and braiding with lathe-turned wooden beads. When only two suspending cords are used, they must be carefully carried around to balance the plant container so the plants will not tip.

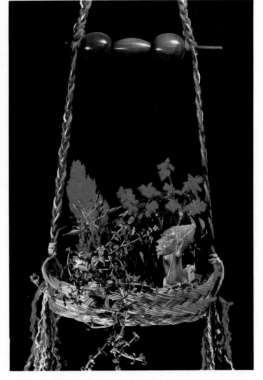

By Tanya Kowalchuk. Crochet over a shaped, painted mannequin form. *Courtesy, artist*

By Arlene Seitzinger. "Two-faced Pot." Polyurethane (foam rubber) cut and carved with small scissors and colored with household dyes and acrylics. The face on the other side of the pot has a different expression with the eyes closed. *Courtesy, artist*

By Stephen Blumrich. Batik hanger with cutout designs assembled. The top cutout is sandwiched between two circles of glass within a metal ring. *Courtesy, artist*

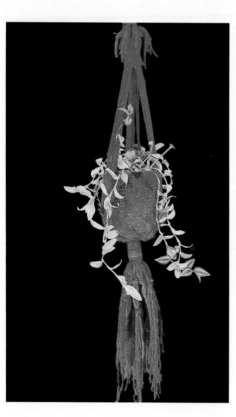

By Dee Menagh. African finger weaving with wool and acrylic yarns.

By Becky Clark. Macramé and wrapping. Square knots are worked in the round for the multiple pot shapes.   *Courtesy, artist*

By Judy Stoup. African finger weaving with natural and synthetic fibers.   *Collection, Raye Malouff*

By Raye Malouff. Basketry coiling with novelty yarns around a gourd.

By Misty Potter. "Talk to Me." Fabric with stenciled design using Versatex fabric dyes and a redwood lath box. *Courtesy, artist*

By Gayle McGinnis. Wrapping and tassels with beads and an odd-shaped basket. *Collection, Diane Powers, San Diego*

By Alice Crowley. Woven flat panels are sewn to make a tube. They can be suspended from a wall hook or set on a table and used for dried flower arrangements or for a lightweight plant.

By Streetcar Glass Works. Stained-glass panels with leading used dimensionally for a plant holder. *Courtesy, Streetcar Glass Works, Lincoln City, Oregon*

By Misty Potter. "Beethoven." Fabric with hand and machine embroidery. Parts are stuffed with fiber fill.

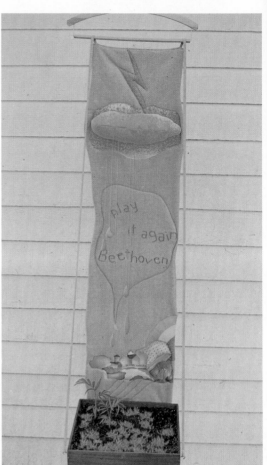

By Dona Meilach. A large wooden bead is used horizontally with square-knot sennits.

By Louise Robbins. Twining with jute and colored wool yarn. Twining is begun at the bottom and the form expanded.

By Laurie Daniells. A tubular woven body holds beautifully cut and finished gourds.

By Gary Cline. Wrapping with some macramé using natural and colored jute.

By Edith Klair. Woven girl plant hanger.  *Photo, Susan Klair*

By Edith Klair. Macramé slings used with an antique pulley.  *Courtesy, artist*

By Susan Smith. Coiled basket container-hanger in mixed yarns with beads.  *Courtesy, artist*

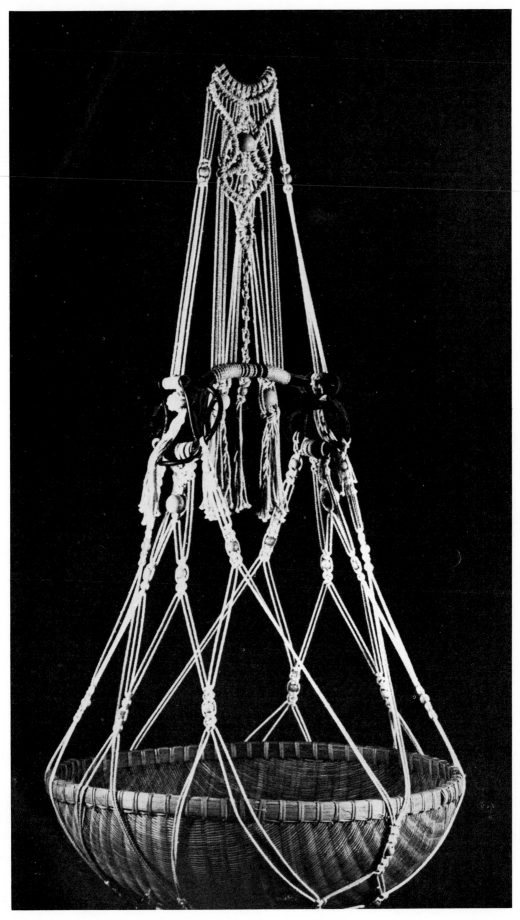

A singletree with two macramé hangers suspended from it. *Courtesy Small Part of the Forest, El Cajon, California*

A pulley can accommodate any type plant and container. *Courtesy, Small Part of the Forest, El Cajon, California*

Edith Klair says old hayblocks, or rope pulleys, are easy to find among the farmlands of Ohio. They are fun to use for hanging pots because when one is pushed up the other goes down. *Photo, Susan Gradual*

Edith Klair uses old barn wood for placing potted plants or flats in different sunny spots as the season dictates. *Photo, Susan Gradual*

The shelf idea is also used by Loay Boland. New or old wood can be used. Each shelf corner has holes so that knots can secure the shelf and prevent it from slipping.

By Betté Hughes. Wire florists' frames (available where plant supplies are sold) provide marvelous frameworks for plant hangers. *Photographed at The Golden Fleece, Laguna Beach, California*

Inside detail of above.

The wire floral frame, similar to that used by Betté Hughes, *left,* has been handled differently by Russell Long. Each wire ring is the holding cord for multiple short strands of white cotton which are simply knotted on with Lark's Heads all around. To achieve the conical shape, the bottom strands are longer than those at the top. The piece measures 46 inches high, 12 inches in diameter. *Photographed at The Plant Palace, Laguna Beach, California*

The sculptural quality of an individual Turk's Head Knot was the inspiration for Kathy Browne's hanging planter. It is supported by a metal plate on the bottom which is bolted to the middle of a 3-foot-by-1½-inch dowel which is wrapped with sisal. A 12-inch ceramic pot was made to the shape of the knot and with a hole in the bottom to accommodate the bolt. Thirty yards of ¾-inch sisal rope was used. *Courtesy, artist*

By Russell Long. Metal hoops are the anchor for Half-Knot Twist sennits. The hoops are secured to a wire basket from which Alternating Square Knots are worked in triangle designs. Soft cotton cable cord. *Photographed at The Plant Palace, Laguna Beach, California*

Bird cage plant hanger by Bill Johnson is 6 feet 1 inch tall and 18 inches in diameter. It is made of specially treated nylon cord so the birds will not nibble on it. *Courtesy, Betty Ann's Handicrafts, San Diego, California*

*Above:*
A light fixture plant hanger by Tom J. Brunelle. The ceramic pot is used upside down, the drain hole accepts the electric wire which is fitted with a lamp socket and the necessary nuts to hold it on each side of the pot. The macramé construction is obvious with the plant cradle at the bottom. Light shining on the nylon cord creates subtle shadows and highlights. *Courtesy, Tom's Green Thumb, Carlsbad, California*

*Right:*
Edith Klair has utilized two ordinary clay flower pots for a lamp. The top pot (upside down) has wire as the anchor for the Half-Knot Twist length in the center that suspends the fixture from a ceiling hook and plugs into the electric wall outlet. Four additional holes in the 7-inch pot bottom are used for anchoring the Half-Knot Twist sennits that suspend the lower pot with plants. *Photo, David Walker*

## LIGHT FIXTURES

A lighted planter can be especially attractive in a dark corner. It lights up the area and dramatizes the plant and the knotting by the shadows it casts. The structure is quite simple. Light fixture parts—sockets, wire, and holding nuts—are available wherever hardware and electric supplies are available. The light can be suspended in any pot used upside down and with a hole in the bottom so the electric cord can be brought through. The pot is held securely by hexagon electrical nuts. Electric cords can be worked into the knotting as anchors for Square Knots, Twists, and Clove Hitches where desired. Cords, available in brown, white, and clear shades, are perfect for the projects.

Bill Johnson carried the idea one step farther and, in addition to the electricity at the top of the hanger, he used a large bowl in the bottom for a fish aquarium (not illustrated). The aerator tubes and electric cords, worked in as anchors for Square Knots, carry the utilities up and down the sides of the hanger body.

## GOURDS WITH MACRAMÉ

The gourd is the hard shelled fruit of a gourd plant. Where the plant is available, people have imaginatively devised a variety of utilitarian and decorative uses for the gourd. It functions as a vessel and utensil for many primitive cultures. African peoples, particularly, have developed uses for the gourd that almost defy the imagination. It furnishes them with work baskets, rattles for scaring birds away from the garden, dippers, bowls, drums, and a variety of musical instruments. Objects are often intricately decorated much the same way we think of decorating pottery and wooden vessels.

Decorating gourds with color and burnt designs is an art practiced for centuries in South and Central America. Fragments of decorated gourds have been excavated from pre-Columbian archeological sites. In Peru, seeds and gourd shells were found in strata dated 3000 B.C. by radiocarbon methods.

Decorative gourds for making useful objects and for artwork are usually available in the fall from farmers' markets, nurseries, gourd farms, and grocery stores and through ads in the craft magazines. All suppliers do not carry them year around; so before you begin chasing from store to store, consult possible sources listed in telephone classified pages.

Gourds have the same working characteristics as wood so that any woodworking tools can be used with them: saws, sharp knives, carving tools, hand drills, wood burning sets, steel wool, and sandpaper. For finishing, you can use natural color varnish, colored acrylic paints, enamels, varnish stains, and shoe polish. Furniture waxes can be used for giving them luster.

When gourds are to be used for planters, they require a substance to make the inside impermeable to moisture. A gourd, being a product of nature, has a tendency to revert to nature if not properly sealed. Very hot melted candle wax, tar or roofing compound, or acrylic resin will seal the inside.

Generally, the following procedures are involved in preparing gourds for use in plant hangers:

**A.** Select a gourd that suggests the shape you visualize for your project; or let the shape of the gourd suggest the idea. Gourds are available in smooth and textured finishes and in many sizes and shapes.

A gourd, cut apart for the plant hanger, *far right*. Always sketch the cutting line with a pencil before actually using a saw. Use a keyhole saw to begin the cut and then you can work with whatever tool will do the job. By Denise Diamond.

The two-part concept can be used as a planter, as shown, or it can be fitted with electric cord and socket and suspended as a hanging planter and lamp. By Denise Diamond.

A textured gourd has only a hole cut out for the plant and it is effective in its simplicity. By Denise Diamond.

**B.** Once you have the gourd of your choice, wash it gently with soapy water and a soft brush. Wipe dry, spread on papers and let it dry thoroughly in a cool, airy place for a minimum of three to four weeks. Another method for drying is to cut the head off and pour water inside. Allow the seeds and contents to rot. Pour the water out and clean away the fleshy materials from the inside. Allow the gourd to dry in the sun until the shell is hard. At this point it is ready to be decorated.

**C.** When the shell is hard and dry, cut the gourd with a saw in any design desired. Remove the seeds and the fibrous material from the inside and rub with fine steel wool if necessary. If there are any mold spots on the outside, wipe off and sand gently. Sandpaper the cut edge. Drill any holes needed for attaching hanging cords, chains, or other material.

**D.** Finish the outside in any creative way. Plain, undecorated gourds can be left in a natural state or covered with any good furniture wax for a nice gloss. Actually, any finish used for wood can be used for finishing the gourd; you might want to give it a coat of varnish before waxing. You can paint the gourd, burn designs in with wood burning tools or the heated point of a screwdriver; surface decoration can also be added using a small hand drill or woodcarver's tools. Unique effects can be achieved by painting the gourd's surface, then cutting back into the natural shade of the gourd as in the examples by Judee DuBourdieu.

**E.** The inside should be finished just like a piece of wood. All pores must be sealed with a prime coat such as thinned house paint, tar, or roofing cement thinned with gasoline or paint thinner. Coat with melted paraffin or candle wax, swishing it around until the entire surface is covered. Colored wax will give the interior an attractive appearance if it is going to show. But a large amount of wax may be needed: much depends on the gourd size. The wax layer should be about ¼ inch thick. Acrylic resin used for boat hulls can be used also.

**F.** Prepare the hanging devices, plant, and use. Gourds should not be hung outside unless in a very protected, dry place.

**G.** The gourd seeds can also be used for beads if they are drilled and strung.

It is possible to grow your own gourds from seeds (look in gardening catalogs). The best time for planting is April or May when the ground is warm. Plant the seeds in full sun, in a well-drained, neutral, fertile soil, and allow ample space for growth. Plant them an inch deep in hills four feet apart with four or five seeds to a hill. Later, thin them to three plants to a hill as they grow very large trailing vines and need lots of room to spread. Growing them on a trellis, wall, or fence is suggested. When the vines are eight or ten feet long, they should be cut to encourage lateral growth.

By the fall, they can be cut with the stems left on, and set out to dry. The creative cycle can begin again with enough gourds to make plant hangers for everyone you know.

A planted gourd photographed at an outdoor plant show illustrates an interesting and practical way to cut a gourd.

58

Three plant hangers by Judee DuBourdieu using gourds, macramé, and beads. Designs are based on Indian rain symbols. "Rainbird–Zuñi Design" was left natural, carved, then areas were stained. The other two gourds were stained and then carved into.

*Left, top:*
Rain Symbol–Santo Domingo Design by Judee DuBourdieu.

*Left, bottom:*
Sik Yatki–Pottery Design by Judee DuBourdieu.

*Right, above:*
Rainbird–Zuñi Design by Judee DuBourdieu.

59

## WRAPPING, TASSELS, AND OTHER KNOTS

An innovative outgrowth of macramé is to isolate wrapping so that it becomes an expressive form unto itself. In the next examples, wrapping with the addition of tassels carries the entire concept of the hanging. Wrapping can be accomplished with any variety of cords. Copper, silver, and gold wire is added also. The wrapped cords can vary from thick to thin, they can contrast color and texture and be combined with floating, unwrapped cords. Study the examples for ideas you can use in your own work.

Many knots other than those associated with macramé can and should be used for enriching a plant hanger or for giving it an entirely different appearance. Doris Fox referred to a book of sailor's knots and the result was her Jacob's Ladder hanger (page 63) made with the same kind of knot boaters used for making ladders to hang over the side of the vessel.

Details of Gary Cline's wrapped hanger, *opposite,* shows, close up, the wrapping, overwrapping, curling, and twisting.

←

Gary Cline's wrapped jute plant hanger in browns and natural colors is richly detailed and subtly shaped and gives an almost baroque appearance with its swirls and curlicues.

Ursy Leuder uses wrapping and feathers with ceramic beads that echo the design in the ceramic pots she makes. *Courtesy, artist*

Gayle McGinnis uses wool and synthetic soft yarns over jute core materials for her wrapped and tasseled piece. The ball-like shapes are wools added on over the original wrapped lengths, then loosely wrapped in the triangular patterns and referred to as "yarn beads." The tassels are held with silver wire and fringed, or unplied. *Photographed at the Del Prado Condominium Model Apartments. Decorator, Brenda Mason* →

John Prater's unusual hanger is made by wrapping and unwrapping. Using very heavy multi-ply jute, he wraps the entire diameter, then unplies sections to create the cradle. He rewraps to bind the sections together again.

Detail of cradle.

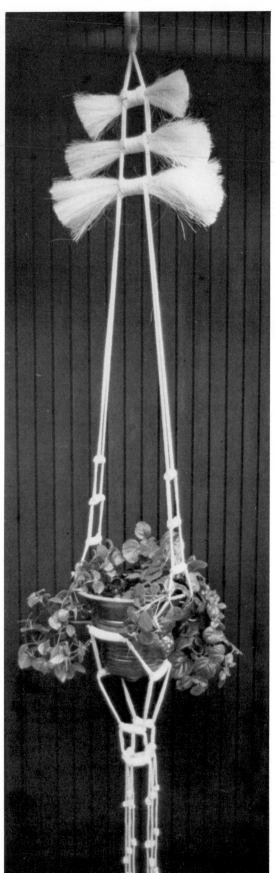

Doris Fox uses #72 seine cord for the planter ropes. The graduated horizontal detailing is unspun sisal (also called box fiber) worked into the Jacob's Ladder Knots at top. *Detail below.* The knots holding the cradle are alternated and made longer than those at the top, then brought together again at the bottom. *Photos, Jo Dendel*

Jacob's Ladder Knot.

A plant hanger by Madge Copeland was woven on a loom as a flat piece of fabric using the Tabby weave in a solid panel for the cradle and the slit technique for top and bottom. The sides were sewn to form a tube, and every other panel was stitched to the top ring, the alternate ones falling to the floor. *Photo, Keith Brewster*

Barbara Hegerle wove three panels separately and gathered the unwoven warp at top and bottom. It is made of Greek handspun wool yarn. Each woven panel is 18 inches long and 5 inches wide. The total piece is 65 inches long. The simple Tabby weave (over one, under one) can be accomplished on a cardboard or frame loom as well as on a conventional loom.

# More Ideas And Techniques With Fibers

There is a tendency to refer to all fiber plant hangers as macramé. Upon close inspection, one becomes aware that many other methods for creating plant hangers are employed—some by themselves and some with macramé. Combining techniques offers variety to finished pieces and a challenge to the creator. For those who may prefer one technique to another, a favorite such as weaving, crochet, and lacemaking can be used and ideas can be culled from examples following. Additional examples in the color sections display batik, tie-dye, and stitchery, and provide more inspirational approaches.

Weaving, as well as the various patterns associated with it, is particularly adaptable to suspended pots. The simple "under one, over one" Tabby weave is the same that you use for darning, or that you used to make pot holders as a child. By extending the warp, the hanging strands can be interestingly designed for function and beauty. Within the weaving category, examples made by twining, an African finger weave, and basketry are shown along with basic directions for developing them. For further forays into any technique refer to the selected bibliography, page 94.

Woven strips can be made on a traditional loom or on a quickly improvised piece of cardboard with notches cut at top and bottom to accept the warp (the vertical threads). With a long weaving needle, the horizontal weft threads are worked back and forth through the warp until a panel results. A wide panel can be made into a tubular shape with a pot cradle fashioned from the warp as shown in several examples. Other examples utilize narrow panels in creative ways to spark ideas on how to proceed using your own ideas.

Materials for weaving, basketry, crochet, lacemaking, and the others are the same as those used for macramé plus softer yarns associated with the weaver's art, such as wools and acrylics. The warp threads and any that will support the weight of the planted pot should be made of nonstretchy materials such as heavy cotton, jute, and sisal.

The weaver, in addition to a loom, notched cardboard, or frame, will require a long weaving needle, a shed stick to separate the warps for easier weaving (a long ruler will suffice), and a comb to beat (push) the weft solidly into place.

## WEAVING

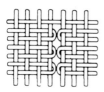

Tabby weave is one over and one under.

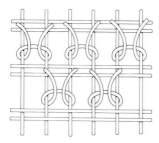

Slit technique allows the panels to be divided.

Weaving frames can be improvised in any way that works for a specific project. A lightweight masonite or wood panel or a picture frame with flat-headed short nails evenly spaced at top and bottom can hold the warp taut while weaving is accomplished. Depending on the length of the warp desired, the yarn may be carried all around the board and taped at beginning and end. After the necessary panel length is woven, the warp is cut at the back to yield the necessary length for the tassel and the body.

For long excess warp, tie each strand onto the board individually, anchor it by winding around the nail twice and then tie at the back to keep the excess length out of your way while weaving. When the panel is completed, untie warps and finish for the head and tail.

Flat woven strips used individually is one approach; the other is to weave a wide panel and sew the selvedges together for a tube. A tube can also be woven "in the round" on a cylinder fitted top and bottom with notches or nails and the warp tied at top and bottom for tension. A cylindrical loom can be a piece of rounded plastic foam, or cardboard tubes found in the discard piles of carpet dealers or manufacturers of cartons.

Ghiordes Knots made with individual fiber lengths in short or long loose ends protruding for a fluffy appearance. Each row is secured with 2 rows of Tabby.

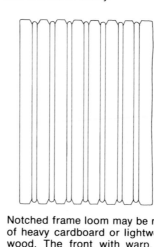

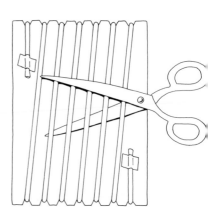

Cylindrical "loom."

Notched frame loom may be made of heavy cardboard or lightweight wood. The front with warp.

The back shows beginning and end and how the warp is cut after the weaving is finished.

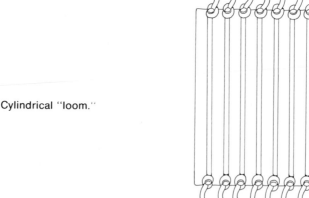

Nails used for holding warp. Tension for weaving is created by tying the warp onto the nails; the long, loose ends would be tied at the back simply to keep them out of the way.

By Laurie Daniells. The panel was woven flat. A wire ring was pushed through the warp loops at the top and the woven panel sewn at the edges to form a tube. Bottom warp ends are wrapped and tied and hanging cords are added. Extra cords are attached to the wire ring to support the pot.

Edith Klair dreamed up this little lady. She is perched on a board and holds a plant in her lap. The piece was woven on a floor loom but it could be done on a backstrap or cardboard loom. The linen warp was fastened to a wood ring; various acrylic nubby yarns were used for weft. *Photo, David Walker*

Laurie Daniells wove a long panel and folded it in half. Actually, the panel is woven together at the right (*bottom*) and open at the left (*top*). The warp threads are knotted to hold the halves together and allowed to dangle for interest. Fur pieces were added using the Ghiordes Knot.

Woven portions within macramé sections are an attractive idea. At right, John Prater illustrates the technique; as simple as pulling the threads through the floating cords using any progression of under and over weaving patterns you like.

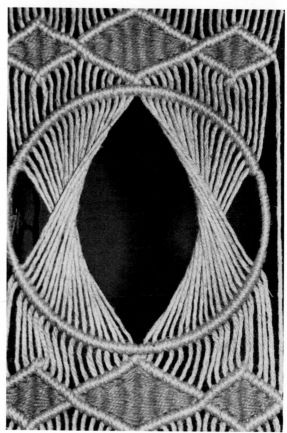

By Sharon La Pierre. Off-loom woven strips are attached to the ceramic pot which has protrusions purposely made for mounting the suspending cords. Pot by Anita Garfein. *Photo, Gerry Sherman*

By Sharon La Pierre. Six woven strips, similar to those used at left, are combined on an antique single-tree. Pot by Joan Hordling. *Photo, Gerry Sherman*

## AFRICAN BRAID AND THE LIBERIAN RICE BAG WEAVE

Peace Corps students and many craftsmen have learned the African technique for finger weaving in the round. The Liberians use the bag for rice, but it has proven versatile as a handbag and now as a plant hanger. The weaving is soft so that the shape is achieved by the form of the pot within.

The weave is accomplished by working with sets of four cords Lark's Headed onto a holding cord pinned around a soft tubular surface such as a roll of paper towels or a large cardboard or Styrofoam® form. Each unit of four cords results in eight ends. The length will depend on the length you wish the finished basket to be, but two yards is good for a practice piece.

The bottom cords can be finished in many decorative ways. They can be gathered and wrapped as shown in the examples, or braided, tasseled, or whatever. Also study the examples on the color pages. If you work with different colors in each grouping, the weaves and diamonds will be easy to follow and will form an intricate pattern.

1

**1.** Assign a number to each cord in each color group. Pick up cords 4 and 5, cross over.

**2.** Pick up cord 3 and cross it over 5.

2

**3.** Pick up cord 6 and weave it under 4 and over 3.

3

**4.** Next pick up cord 2 and weave it under, over, and under the woven cords, as shown. Then pick up cord 7 and weave it in. Do the same with 1 and then 8.

The progression is simply to take a cord from the left side and weave it under those in the center; then pick up one from the right side and weave it.

That is the basic African braid weave. To form the weave into a tubular shape, Lark's Head additional groups of four cords all around the tubular form and weave each group; then work the groups together.

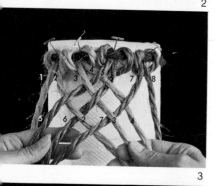

4

**5.** To work the groups together, join the points between them. Pick up the top cord of the unit on right hand side. Cross it over the top cord of the unit to the left of it. Continue weaving until all cords from the right have been woven with those at the left and a diamond shape is formed. Continue working in this way all around and until you reach the desired length.

5

The rice bag plant holder shown in the color section appears like this when flat. By Judy Stoup. *Collection, Raye Malouff*

Dee Menagh's purple and red wool rice bag hanging in progress. The yarn is pinned to a roll of paper towels. Various wool and synthetic yarns are used for texture and color variation.

Sisal and wool rice bag hanger by Judy Stoup. *Collection, Raye Malouff*

**TWINING** Twining is usually associated with weaving. It is finding its way into many types of fiber arts, and a few people have already applied the process to plant hangers. Actually, twining is believed to be older than weaving and examples date back to 2000 B.C. in Peru and, later, throughout South America.

In weaving, the weft is worked over and under the warp so that the warp is exposed. In twining, a doubled cord is worked simultaneously over and under each weft so that the weft is <u>enclosed.</u> When thick cords are used twining goes very quickly; form develops rapidly once you achieve the rhythm required to twist the weft between each warp.

Basic twining is shown. There are many variations possible such as two twists between each warp, varying the twists, combining twining with counter twining, and so forth. After you practice twining, you will be able to see how color can be controlled by the direction of the twist, by using two colors simultaneously, or making stripes by alternating the twist over a specified number of warps. For the hangers, the twining is begun starting from the top over a series of folded warps. For additional twining methods refer to books on weaving and basketry.

A twined basket begun from the top will have loose ends at the bottom that can be finished as in macramé. A smaller form can be made, turned upside down and assembled into the top form so that a closed bottom results. Expanding a form is accomplished by adding in folded warps. To narrow a form, skip warps and let them fall within the basket or twine over two warps at a time. The examples shown will give you several ideas.

Twining involves using a doubled weft and crossing it once between each warp; each cord reverses its position every warp. When working around a tubular shape for a basket, the direction of the crossover should be consistent each time for a uniform pattern. To change the appearance of the design, the weft can be crossed in the opposite direction every other row. You must mark the beginning of a row with an extra thread tied on so you know where you want to begin the change each time.

Twining packed solidly by pushing up the rows with a weaver's beater, or a comb.

Cut several lengths of cord for the warp. Fold them in half. The length of the folded cord will be the length of your basket but allow enough extra for finishing. Make as many loops as you need for the circumference of the basket desired. Fold a length of weft cord (work with a strand about 2 yards long) and place around one leg of the loop. Cross and twine over the second leg.

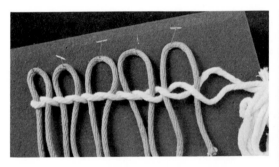

Until you get the rhythm of twining, it is sometimes easier to begin the first row with the loops pinned onto a board. Each warp is enclosed; the weft crosses in the same direction between each warp.

To form the warps into the tubular shape, continue twining in the second row by bringing the first leg around and following through in the round.

Continue twining for as many rows as desired. Always pack the twining solidly by pushing each row up with your fingers or a large-toothed comb.

To make the shape wider, add doubled cords into the work decoratively and evenly all around. A single strand could be added, too, but you must be careful not to pull it out.

Twined hanging baskets by Louise Robbins attest to the value of twining as a technique for making different plant hangers. She begins the form from a nucleus of looped cords used at the bottom and then adds warp cords as she needs them to enlarge the form. Some of the remaining warp cords are used to suspend the basket, others are treated decoratively; some are wrapped and allowed to hang, or looped back into the form. The warp is jute, the wefts are Greek and Mexican handspun wools. They vary in height from 24 to 28 inches.

By Louise Robbins. *Collection, Martha Roche, Houston, Texas*

**Twining and Macramé**  Dee Nemeth combines macramé methods with twining for the planter developed over a glass bowl (right), shown in three views. The piece can be started over a beach ball to make it lighter and less apt to break during construction. But before the top and bottom are assembled, the glass bowl must be inserted.

A holding cord is placed in a circle (you can start this on a knotting board, too), and vertical cords are doubled and mounted with Lark's Head Knots all around the circle. One row of Vertical Clove Hitches is made on each cord. The spokes of the Lark's Headed cords become the warp for twining.

For the interesting spacing, the ends of the warp are looped and a Vertical Clove Hitch made to hold them. Another set of cords is looped through these (see side view, *right*) and then twining is continued for the bottom portion. Some of the cords are extended upward and wrapped for suspending the hanger.

## BASKET COILING

The easy-to-learn coiling technique used by basket makers of many cultures is now being adapted to fiber arts. Baskets, normally associated with wood splits and natural grasses, can readily be made with easy-to-find materials such as jute, wool, sisal, cotton rope, and other materials. Coiled basket hangers are a challenge to create, and the coiling technique adapts beautifully to macramé, weaving, and crochet so that combinations of many fiber methods can enhance a hanger. The more techniques one knows, the more challenging it can be to give a hanger a unique appearance, and project it out of the ordinary.

The following demonstration illustrates the basics of basket coiling using the Lazy Stitch and the Figure 8 Stitch. For additional basket-making ideas with fibers, refer to *A Modern Approach to Basketry* by Dona Z. Meilach (Crown Publishers, N.Y.).

Use a heavy, dull-finish cord for the core (slick-finish nylon, rayon, and similar cords tend to slide and are difficult to work with), a thinner material for wrapping, and a needle with a large eye for the wrapping cord. You will require much more wrapping than core material.

1

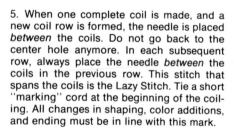

2

**BASKET COILING**

1. Taper the core material and begin to wrap about 1½ inches from the end.

2. Fold the wrapped end and bring the cord over as shown. Tighten to form a circle with a small hole. Wrap around both cords once.

3. Bring the needle through the center hole . . .

4. . . . and over the top cord. Wrap the top cord only three times and bring the needle through the hole again and over the top cord. As you work, form the rope into a circular coil.

5. When one complete coil is made, and a new coil row is formed, the needle is placed *between* the coils. Do not go back to the center hole anymore. In each subsequent row, always place the needle *between* the coils in the previous row. This stitch that spans the coils is the Lazy Stitch. Tie a short "marking" cord at the beginning of the coiling. All changes in shaping, color additions, and ending must be in line with this mark.

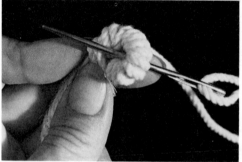

3

4

5

6

7

8

9

10

11

12

13

6. The Figure 8 Stitch is formed by bringing the needle between the coils, over the core material and between the coil again before inserting it into the row beneath and proceeding with the wraps. The wrap actually forms an 8 between the core rope. The stitch does not show on the outside of the coils as does the Lazy Stitch. It is hidden between them.

7. When your wrap cord shortens, add a new piece by first laying the end of the new length along the core and wrapping it in with the short end of the old length.

8. Then lay the end of the old length on the cord, pick up the new length, wrap in the old and continue to work with the new length.

9. To shape the basket, simply place the core wherever you want it to move. For a sharp 90° basket side, place the core on top of the base; begin the shaping at the point of movement marked by the extra cord tied on.

10. To add colors, work them in the same way you would add on cords or for short lengths. Add the new cord onto the core and keep the initial color under the new cord and pick it up and use it as needed.

11. To end the basket: Taper the core material so the end will be even with the point of movement. Wrap a loop of extra cord along the core as shown, leaving the ends protruding.

12. Continue wrapping and when you reach the end, put your needle through the loop. Remove the needle.

13. Pull the loose ends of the extra cord so it buries the end of your wrap beneath the coil. Remove the extra cord. If necessary, add a dab of white glue to hold the tip.

Coiled and crocheted hanger by Sharon La Pierre. Eight feet long (see detail of coiling around a gourd, *right*). *Photo, Gerry Sherman*

Cactus environment by Jaye Lawrence is completely coiled and suspended by a Half-Knot Twist sennit. The shape of the hanger repeats the shape and texture of the plant. The piece is made of jute, handspun yarns, and spun dog hair.

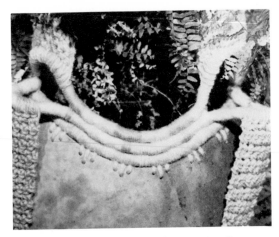

Detail of the coiling and crochet construction on a gourd by Sharon La Pierre.

Coiled basket hanger with beads by Susan Smith. *Courtesy, artist*

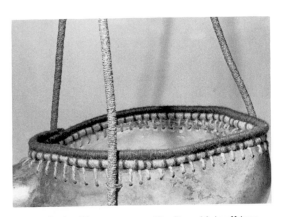

Detail of coiling on a gourd by Raye Malouff (see color pages for complete basket).

Coiling on a gourd by Jude Martin. Wool yarns over a jute core.

## CROCHET, LACE, AND NETTING

Probably all the ways people manipulate fibers and yarns can be adpated to plant hangers, as shown in the examples on these pages. Sometimes all that is needed are imagination and a willingness to experiment.

Sally Davidson and Carol Hoffman, both accomplished crocheters, used soft fibers readily workable with a crochet hook to create the hangers on this page. Sally's piece connects directly to holes in the pot; it begins at the top with a ring and employs the double crochet stitch in the round. The weight of the pot pulls the piece down so the stitches separate.

Carol Hoffman's crochet hangers are intricately developed and rounded out with hoops at top and bottom; the left piece has additional hoops in the center because crochet does not retain the stiffness and form of macramé. Pots are placed in the top, or within the hanger so that the plants can grow out through the holes which also supply light.

Kaethe Kliot, well known for her contemporary approach to bobbin lace, used the twists and braids of that technique and developed plant hangers suspended from branches.

Netting that you can make, or buy ready made, can be an attractive holder for plants that are small and unpotted, such as these desert varieties that thrive on pieces of wood. It is a nice treatment for an outdoor semiroofed area where light comes in. and when you want to camouflage the structure.

Crocheted plant hangers by Carol Maree Hoffman. *Left,* jute, 34 inches long; *right,* rose-colored wool, 34 inches long. *Photo, Laura Benson*

Crocheted hanger by Sally Davidson. *Photo, artist*

Bobbin lace plant hangers by Kaethe Kliot.
*Photos, Jules Kliot*

Netting with plants hooked on and suspended.
*Jamul Gardens, California*

A leather pot hanger by Scott B. Nelles is a handsome accessory and a unique idea in English bridle leather. See the demonstration on pages 86–87.

# Planter

# "Pot" Pourri

As the hanging planter continues to invade the spaces around us, it is inevitable that the devices for displaying them pique the imaginations of designers. The examples in this chapter are only a hint at the variety that is emerging. Many are created on a large scale for use in public spaces; these ideas can be scaled down for homes, offices, restaurants, and wherever a touch of "pot" pourri can be used.

Two uses of leather in entirely different ways are offered by Scott Nelles and Charles Houston. Stained glass planters as shelves and boxes and for environments for terrariums (see color pages) are colorful and decorative.

Woodworkers and metalworkers can apply their skills to transcend the ordinary as in the plant hangers by Al Garvey and Richard Parkin. The designers of the huge hangers in Chicago's brilliantly decorated "Warehouse" on North Clark Street are not known, but their good taste can be emulated in smaller spaces where desired.

Obviously, there are no rules, no one way to hang a plant. The only criterion may be that the plant should be hung where it enhances the decor, where it receives adequate light for growth, and where it can be readily watered without dripping on furnishings or on the heads of patrons below the hangings. Whether the plants should be subordinate to the hanging or the hanger be subordinate to the plant is a question that only your taste and preference can answer.

## PROCEDURES FOR MAKING A LEATHER POT

Scott B. Nelles demonstrates the general steps required to fashion a leather pot hanger. He uses a sturdy 10-to-12-oz. English bridle leather to give the piece structural strength and strength of appearance. For more detailed leather-working techniques, refer to the books listed on page 94.

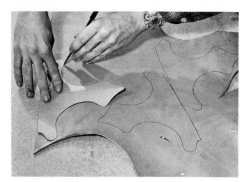

1

1. A paper or cardboard pattern is used to trace the outline of the individual pieces onto the leather.

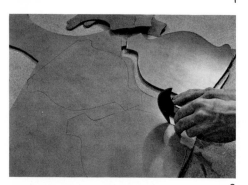

2

2. The pattern pieces are laid out to utilize the leather's best quality and not waste portions of the leather. The pieces are cut out with a half-moon leather cutting knife.

3. The pieces are dyed to the desired tones with leather dye applied with a cloth. The leather is dampened before dyeing; coloring may also be accomplished after the leather has been soaked.

3

4. The leather is soaked in water for about half an hour to make it pliable and moldable.

5. The edge seams are creased by pounding them over with a hammer . . .

6. . . . and then incising a line at the bend. This defines the seam from the planter body. The pieces are allowed to dry for about 24 hours.

6

4

5

7. The dried pieces have retained the shape given them when wet. They are now ready to be glued with a leather cement.

8. The decorative portions and the sides can be hand sewn using a punch and leather awl. If available, a heavy duty sewing machine can be used.

9. After sewing, the piece is again soaked in water but allowed only to partially dry so it can be further molded and formed without reverting to its original shape. Shaping can be done with the hands and with simple tools.

10. When the planter has completely dried, Scott lines the inside with a coat of melted brewer's pitch, which waterproofs the interior in the same way ancient leather bottles were coated. One can also use roofing tar or melted paraffin.

11. Finishing touches are given to the exterior; seams and corners are smoothed, edges are dyed and burnished. A protective coating of clear lacquer is applied over all and the straps are added.

12. The straps are designed to repeat the stitching and detailing in the pot. *Photos, Scott B. Nelles*

7

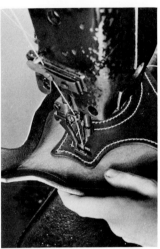

8

9

10

11

12

Leather plant hangers by Charles Houston are combined with ceramic pots, bones, weather-smoothed pieces of wood, and antique parts. Mr. Houston creates the pots himself. *Photos, Bill Bayer*

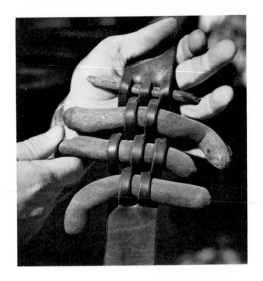

Assembled items for hanging plants can be attractive, different, and inexpensive to create. A woven basket from an old lamp, a seashell wind chime, and the pot beneath brighten a window overlooking the city. By J. D. Griggs.

Use a scale, antique or modern, for displaying plants outdoors or in the corner of a kitchen or den. By Beverly Stefanski.

A planter made with materials from the sewing counter costs under a dollar excluding the basket. "Straps" are sold for trimming clothing; a half skein of acrylic has been made into tassels fastened with the strapping. By Sue Stanli.

Stained glass hanging planters are becoming increasingly popular and can be made as shelves or boxes, or pieces of the glass can be incorporated into macramé hangings. They add color and sparkle wherever they are used. By Claire Ravizza. *Photo, Sally Davidson*

Large spaces can accommodate hangers made to scale. At Chicago's "Warehouse," the three tiers of metal rings held together with marine rope span two floors and support many plants. A smaller version could be used where applicable.

By Richard Parkin. Forged copper parts set in and onto a wooden beam. *Photo, C. L. McKinnon*

Plant stand by Al Garvey is whimsical. The arm and leg positions can be changed. Various kinds of carved woods.

A dried log uprighted and fitted with a flower pot at top can also support plants around the exterior for use in a garden or mounted on a wall. *Courtesy, Small Part of the Forest*

A boat pulley that once hoisted heavy cargoes is now put to restful use supporting wood beams at opposing angles from which plants are suspended in interesting balanced arrangement. At the "Warehouse," Chicago.

# For Further Reference

**BOOK REFERENCES**

The selected list of books below will help you discover additional ideas within each technique category.

Ashley, Clifford W. *The Ashley Book of Knots.* New York: Doubleday & Co., Inc., 1944.

Dendel, Esther Warner. *African Fabric Crafts.* New York: Taplinger Publishing Co., 1974.

James, George Wharton. *Indian Basketry* and *How To Make Indian and Other Baskets.* New York: Henry Malkan, 1903. Facsimile Edition, Glorieta, New Mexico: Rio Grande Press, 1970.

Kliot, Kaethe and Jules. *Bobbin Lace: Form by the Twisting of Cords.* New York: Crown Publishers, 1973.

Meilach, Dona Z. *Contemporary Batik and Tie-Dye.* New York: Crown Publishers, Inc., 1973.

————. *Contemporary Leather.* Chicago: Henry Regnery Co., 1971.

————. *Macramé Accessories.* New York: Crown Publishers, Inc., 1972.

————. *Macramé: Creative Design in Knotting.* New York: Crown Publishers, Inc. 1971.

————. *A Modern Approach to Basketry with Fibers and Grasses.* New York: Crown Publishers, Inc., 1974.

————. *Soft Sculpture and Other Soft Art Forms.* New York: Crown Publishers, Inc., 1974.

Meilach, Dona Z., and Snow, Lee Erlin. *Weaving Off-Loom.* Chicago: Henry Regnery Co., 1973.

Stanli, Sue. *Basketry with Fibers.* San Francisco: Eveready Superior Products, 1976.

**CORD SIZE AND WEIGHT CHART**

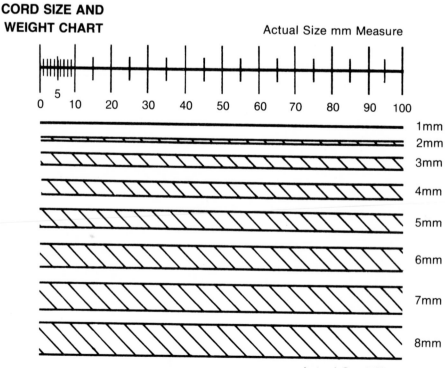

Actual Size mm Measure

Actual Cord Sizes

# Index